Ashbel Woodward

Statue of Colonel Thomas Knowlton

Ceremonies at the unveiling

Ashbel Woodward

Statue of Colonel Thomas Knowlton
Ceremonies at the unveiling

ISBN/EAN: 9783337248215

Printed in Europe, USA, Canada, Australia, Japan

Cover: Foto ©ninafisch / pixelio.de

More available books at **www.hansebooks.com**

STATUE OF COLONEL THOMAS KNOWLTON CEREMONIES AT THE UNVEILING

HARTFORD, CONN.

PRESS OF THE CASE, LOCKWOOD & BRAINARD COMPANY

1895

CONTENTS

Resolved by this Assembly, That the Commission of Sculpture be and is hereby authorized to have prepared and constructed a suitable memorial consisting of a companion piece to the statue of Nathan Hale, or other suitable memorial, to be placed in the Capitol or erected upon the Capitol grounds, to commemorate the gallant service and heroic death, in the war of the Revolution, of Col. Thomas Knowlton of Ashford; *provided,* that the expense therefor shall not exceed seven thousand five hundred dollars; and the sums expended by said Commission under this resolution shall be paid by the Comptroller upon the presentation of proper vouchers therefor.

Approved, June 14, 1893.

CEREMONIES

THE ceremonies were held in the Hall of the House of Representatives in Hartford, Nov. 13, 1895, the chairman of the Commission of Sculpture* in the chair, in the presence of a very large and distinguished audience, the Governor and his staff, the State officers, the descendants of Colonel Knowlton, representatives of the Historical Societies of Connecticut and of New Haven, and other invited guests. After the invocation of the Divine Blessing by the Rev. Joseph H. Twichell of Hartford, followed the

PRESENTATION BY CHARLES DUDLEY WARNER

Ladies and Gentlemen, Governor Coffin : —

THE Legislature of 1893 appropriated the sum of seven thousand five hundred dollars for the erection of a bronze statue of Colonel Thomas Knowlton. The suggestion of this act of justice to one of the heroes of the Revolution of whom the state has most reason to be proud came from the descendants of Colonel Knowlton. The execution of this mandate fell to the Commission of Sculpture* under the law creating that body. The Commission asked

---

* The members are Charles Dudley Warner, chairman; Alfred E. Burr, Henry W. Farnam, Francis Goodwin, Kirk H. Leavens, and J. Q. A. Stone.

Mr. E. S. Woods of Hartford to prepare a model for the statue, and when this was made to their satisfaction a contract was given to him for the statue and pedestal. The bronze was cast by Mr. M. H. Mosman of Chicopee, Mass., and the granite pedestal, designed by Mr. Henry Bryant, was made by the New England Granite Company. It is a beautiful piece of work.

The statue is eight feet in height, the plinth four inches, and the pedestal eight feet, making the monument sixteen feet four inches high. Upon the pedestal is a bronze tablet, reciting, without eulogy, the deeds which justify the erection of the statue by the state. The monument has been placed at the southeast corner of the Capitol, in a position to show it to advantage from most points of view, without dwarfing it by contrast with the building.

The object has been to present within the allowable limits of art an historic figure, representative of the time and of the soldier who died in action. The only authority for the likeness is in Trumbull's portrait of Knowlton in his famous picture of the battle of Bunker Hill. In the judgment of the Commission the statue is worthy of the hero and of the conspicuous position it occupies.

I have said that the tablet records his deeds. The character and genius of the man will be unfolded in the historical address by Mr. P. H. Woodward, who by birth and study is especially·fitted for the work. Colonel Knowlton was a great man. Judged by what he did and by what his rare talents promised, I doubt if the state has produced a greater military genius or a more unselfish patriot. The official recognition of his services and his great qualities comes late, but his fame is permanent and it will increase, for it is of the sort of heroism that the people take to heart long after the flags are folded and the drums are silent.

I am authorized to extend to the descendants of Colonel Knowlton a cordial welcome to these ceremonies, and to assure them that in honoring the memory of Colonel Knowlton the state is conscious that one of the best legacies of an honorable name is a worthy and patriotic posterity.

With the unveiling, the labor of the Commission ceases, and they commit the statue of Colonel Thomas Knowlton to the keeping of the state, whose chief treasure is its great citizens.

ACCEPTANCE BY GOVERNOR O. VINCENT COFFIN

Mr. Chairman and Friends : —

THE state is under many and great obligations to you and the other members of the Commission of Sculpture for the faithful and painstaking way in which the duties of the commissioners have been hitherto discharged. In no one of the many instances in which your services have been required have you had a more interesting or more important work placed under your care than when you were charged with the duty of obtaining the statue we unveil to-day.

It affords me great pleasure to add that in no

other case have your efforts been more gratifyingly successful. Doubtless you may have thought at times that there has not been manifested that general and responsive interest you desire in the results of your attempts to have this splendid capitol and its beautiful grounds adorned in a manner appropriate to their merits and befitting the dignity and history of the state. But in these days of the renaissance of popular interest in the heroes of our earlier times, especially those of the Revolutionary period, you are certain to have widely extended and grateful appreciation of the excellent judgment and patriotic purpose evidenced by the notable and singularly timely addition to our art treasures which you now tender.

As the years go on there is to be, I am sure, a rapidly increasing interest in our early history and in the men and women whose words and deeds have covered its pages with glory.

We do well, then, to place in conspicuous position upon these grounds this statue of the brave and patriotic Knowlton, and I accept it with great pleasure in behalf of the people of the state.

HISTORICAL ADDRESS.

By P. Henry Woodward.

BETWEEN the lives of Col. Thomas Knowlton and of his grand-nephew Gen'l Nathaniel Lyon may be traced a close parallel. Born of a common stock and reared in the same neighborhood, both entered the military service in boyhood, one as a volunteer in the Old French and Indian war, and the other as a cadet at West Point; both were brave and skillful soldiers; both fell in battle early in the struggles undertaken respectively to establish and to preserve the republic; and both were borne onward to heroic deeds by an ardent belief in the ideas for which they died.

A deep interest in Col. Knowlton, joined to a tender regard for his memory, falls as an inheritance to the speaker. Among the papers of my father *

---

* Dr. Ashbel Woodward, late of Franklin, Conn., from boyhood took great delight in genealogical and antiquarian research. Among his early comrades were Capt. Miner Knowlton, a graduate of and professor at West Point, Danford Knowlton, brother of Miner, both grand-nephews of Col. Thomas Knowlton, and William W. Marcy, who married the only daughter of Thomas Knowlton, Jr. They were untiring in efforts to collect facts in regard to Col. Knowlton and his associates. Nearly forty years ago the papers were all turned over to Doctor Woodward. He published a memoir of Col. Knowlton in the New England Historical and Genealogical Register for January 1861, and a genealogy of the family in the number for the following October.

This coterie of inquirers felt that scant justice had been done to one of the bravest and ablest soldiers of the Revolution, and impressed their convictions upon the youth who listened to their talk. In 1893 the were statements, taken from the lips of soldiers who shared in the fight, of the part performed by Col. Knowlton and his command at the battle of Bunker Hill. Though too young to grasp the drift of the talk I was present at various interviews with survivors of the Revolution, and listened as if to echoes from a remote or unreal world. In these papers, too, are outlined marches through frontier solitudes where, as hostile forces collide, the stillness of the forest is cruelly broken by the shrieks of savages and the crash of musketry.

ANCESTRY.

John Knowlton, the ancestor of Col. Thomas of the sixth generation, is found in Ipswich, Mass., as early as 1639. About the middle of the century a branch of the family moved to Ashford, Conn., from West Boxford, Mass., where Thomas was born in November, 1740. William, the emigrant, brought with him a large family. He bought a farm not far from the village church, the first recorded deed bearing date 1748.

time to ask for recognition seemed to have come. At the January session of the Connecticut legislature Hon. Edward S. Cleveland, Senator from Hartford, a native of Windham County, was chairman of the joint select committee on Capitol Furniture and Grounds. His uncle, ex-Governor Chauncey F. Cleveland, and others had often expressed in his presence an ardent admiration for Col. Knowlton. Hence when the matter was brought to his attention the senator, already convinced of the justice of the proposal, earnestly approved and advocated the resolution providing for a statue. A number of veterans from the Connecticut Historical Society appeared before the committee to urge the passage of the measure.

ADVENTURES IN FRENCH AND INDIAN WARS.

In the last French and Indian war, at the age
of sixteen, Thomas enlisted as a private under
Captain Durkee, serving till the conquest of Canada
brought peace. In August, 1758, he took part in
the battle of Wood Creek. Here this lad, not yet
eighteen, met with a succession of bloody encounters
and hair-breadth escapes, which, as told around the
winter firesides of Windham County, often formed
part of the evening entertainment for children who
long since grew old and passed away.

A detachment of five or six hundred men under
Majors Putnam and Rogers were scouring the
country east of Lake George. Coming upon a camp
which bore marks of recent occupancy, and finding
sundry utensils secreted near by, they held the
ground to await the expected return of the enemy.
Some of our people fishing in a canoe met two French
boats, when both parties hurried in opposite directions
to sound the alarm. Breaking camp the English
started again through the forest. The position of
the next encampment was disclosed by the incautious
conduct of two officers who engaged in target practice.
Near by was hovering the French partisan Molang
with a force of equal strength and with superior
knowledge of the ground. The following day, as
the provincials in single file were picking their way
through the thick growth of underwood, the whiz
of bullets and the warwhoop suddenly betrayed the
nearness of the enemy. Ever on the alert for such
emergencies, from the shelter of trees and brush they

opened fire in return. Soon the lines became en-
tangled with each other and the fight drifted into a
succession of duels between persons and squads.
Early in the contest Knowlton espied an Indian
creeping stealthily through the brakes. He shot
the savage, reloaded and started to secure his scalp
for a trophy. All at once he found himself surround-
ed. Armed men seemed to spring up out of the
earth. Perhaps from fear of hitting friends the
warriors did not fire, but beckoned to him to surrender. Casting a swift glance along the circle, he shot
one of the group, and plunging into the thicket,
escaped.

Later Knowlton met in a small opening a stalwart
Frenchman. The muskets of both missed. They
grappled in a trial of personal strength. The youth
was overpowered and thrown. At this juncture a
comrade rushed to his support when the Frenchman
begged for quarter. The old and not always trusty
flint lock was reprimed, and as they were moving
away the prisoner made a sudden break for liberty,
when a shot from Knowlton ended his flight and life
together.

AT THE SIEGE OF HAVANA.

In July, 1759, Knowlton shared in the capture
of Ticonderoga. In 1762 under Gen'l Lyman he
joined the expedition for the reduction of Havana.
August 13th the city surrendered, but tropical diseases
had so wasted the ranks of the provincials that but
a sorry fragment of the contingent from Connecticut was spared to return to their native hills. On

the homeward voyage an English officer whose insolence while in liquor Knowlton had resented, invited him to settle the difficulty by duel, but, either from consciousness of wrong or from prudence, withdrew the challenge with an apology before coming to land. Greatly to the disgust of the colonies, the next year the crown restored to Spain its costly conquests in Cuba.

In March, 1760, Knowlton was appointed ensign of the 3d company, 1st regiment, Connecticut forces; in March, '61, ensign of the 10th company, Robert Durkee, Captain; and in March, '62, second lieutenant of the 10th company, Hugh Ledlie, Captain.

MARRIAGE.

Returning home at the close of summer campaigns, the youthful soldiers of the period did not permit the alarms of war to exclude love-making and matrimony. April 5, 1759, Knowlton married Anna, daughter of Sampson Keyes of Ashford, but did not settle into domestic repose till after the siege of Havana. He then returned to the plow and the spade, drifting tranquilly with the tide till the blood of Lexington opened a new era in the progress of humanity.

CHANGE OF FEELING TOWARD ENGLAND.

During the dozen years of peaceful sowing and reaping a great change had been wrought in the temper of the colonies toward Great Britain, due, from the colonial point of view, in part to odious fiscal regulations and in part to the arrogance of English officers on duty in America.

The preliminary duel was fought with Massachusetts. In that colony the tyranny of the Stuarts had evoked a chronic habit of. non-compliance with the wishes of the crown. Her people, called as the elect from the morning of time to bear the ark which none but Israel might touch, and ever waspish toward aggression, presented a sharp, active, and acrid sting to the measures proposed for their amendment by a succession of royal rulers. The retaliatory acts of the ministry led up to the Boston Tea Party and the night march to Concord.

In the light of her history it is hard to see why Connecticut adopted so ardently the contention of her neighbor. From the outset she had studiously avoided controversy with the crown. Valuing things above words, she never dropped the substance to clutch at the shadow. Eluding observation while pursuing with resolute purpose a well-defined policy, she pushed ahead vigorously in periods of calm, and when kings grew meddlesome waited silently in serene patience for a change in the royal temper. By the prudence of her leaders she became from the start a self-governing republic, as free almost under the Georges as she is to-day. Her internal condition was, perhaps, more changed by the constitution of 1818 than by the revolution of 1776.

After 1760 a gradual change took place in the subjects which engrossed popular attention. Deductions respecting the moral government of the universe, drawn with merciless logic from premises accepted with no apparent hesitation — subtleties on which in the absence of science and a varied literature the intellect of New England had long been sharpened, gave way to the study of the British constitution and of natural rights. Arguments winged with the eloquence of an Otis and a Henry both convinced and inflamed a willing people, preparing the way for the entry of a new nation so soon as the conflict should move onward from the platform to the battle-field.

AT HOME.

On leaving the army in 1762, Colonel Knowlton lived in Ashford on his farm of four hundred acres, where eight children were born to him. At the age of thirty-three he was elected selectman, and it was deemed a notable occurrence that one so young should be honored by his fellow citizens with this distinguished mark of confidence. "Old men for council," was the maxim of our prudent fathers. He is described at this time as about six feet tall, slender but sinewy, of dark hair, blue eyes and fair complexion, erect and handsome, affable and courteous, with a winsomeness that drew friends and a constancy that held them.

Scrupulous in conduct, he had little sympathy with the prevalent intolerance. It is related that, attracted on one occasion by the crowd around the village whipping post — then an instrument of grace — he noticed the omission from the sentence of the usual clause requiring the lash to be applied to the bare back, and threw his own overcoat over the shoulders of the delinquent to lighten the pain.

STORM SIGNALS.

September 1, 1774, General Gage seized and removed a quantity of powder stored by the provincials at Cambridge. Amid the excitement and wrath provoked by the act, a report was started that the British had fired upon our people. Flying by word of mouth, as rumors do, the story reached General Putnam at Pomfret the morning of the 3d. This he first reduced to writing and sent on with his initials attached. Through Norwich, New London, New Haven, New York, Philadelphia, and the regions beyond, the story sped onward. Within a few hours thousands of men in Connecticut alone were ready to march under arms to avenge the supposed wrong. Everywhere the news called forth similar proofs of patriotism. Putnam with four comrades hurried on horseback toward Boston and reached Douglass before learning that the alarm was false. Galloping homeward and sending out couriers to convey counter tidings he thus stopped several detachments already well advanced on the road. Whether the story was started through mistake, or intentionally to test the public temper, the response afforded convincing proof that the masses were ready for armed resistance.

Shortly after on the 9th of September a convention of delegates from New London and Windham counties met at Norwich. It voted a number of recommendations with the view of putting the militia of

Eastern Connecticut on an effective war footing. At
the October session the General Assembly enacted
that prior to the ensuing May each military company
in the colony shall be exercised twelve half days in
the use of arms. The several towns were ordered to
provide double the quantities of powder, balls, and
flints before required by law. In the swelling flood
of enthusiasm resolves of conventions and acts of leg-
islatures served but to give a more solemn sanction to
the spontaneous movements of the hour.

WINDHAM COUNTY IN ARMS.

On Wednesday, April 19, 1775, occurred the fight
at Lexington. At ten o'clock A.M. a post was dis-
patched from Watertown, Mass., to Worcester, to convey tidings of the expedition and to alarm the people.
Early the next morning the news crossed the Connecticut line and before night had spread over Windham
county. Work was dropped. Friday was given up to
new but intense activities. Officers rode hither and
thither to call out their men and make ready for the
coming march. Wives and daughters ran bullets and
cooked rations.

Knowlton hastened to the rendezvous of the Ashford Company on the eastern border of the town and,
though long out of service, was chosen by acclamation
to the vacant* office of captain. The place sought the

---

* Lieut. Reuben Marcy, a man of high character and held in high
esteem for personal virtues, was acting commander before the election of
Knowlton. His father, Edward Marcy, had been a lieutenant and later a
captain in the French and Indian wars, but the son had seen no service.
After the return from Cambridge he resigned. The next year he raised
and commanded the Fourth company of Colonel Chester's regiment, tak-

2

man because in soldierly qualities and gifts of leader-
ship he stood pre-eminent. His wife, who preferred
peace with her husband to aught that war could win
without him, for once found his heart hardened
against entreaties and tears.

Without delay the command hurried over the hills
to Pomfret, where the Fifth Regiment, Jedediah
Elderkin, Colonel, had been ordered to rendezvous.
Sunday morning other companies arrived from Mans-
field, Coventry, and Windham. Early in the afternoon the officers held a council. Embarrassed most
by the size of the sudden outpour, they voted to take
one-fifth from the ten companies present and to send
the other four-fifths home to await future orders. For
special fitness the Ashford Company was selected
entire and to that extent the draft upon the others
was reduced. So quickly were arrangements pushed
that by five o'clock the same afternoon the detachment under Major Thomas Brown and Captain
Knowlton set out for Cambridge, Lieutenant-Colonel
Experience Storrs accompanying them as far as Dudley. This was the first organized body of troops from
beyond her borders to join the Massachusetts forces
around Boston.

Levies collected at an hour's notice were not prepared to enter upon a long campaign. Accordingly,
after a few days the Connecticut troops returned

ing part in the campaign of 1776 around New York city. It is a curious
fact that Daniel Knowlton, a brother of Colonel Thomas, and a fearless
and famous scout, joined the company of Captain Marcy, of which he was
ensign. In August Daniel was detached with others to make up Knowlton's Rangers. Captain Marcy died January 14, 1806.

home to arrange their affairs for the serious business of war.

BATTLE OF BUNKER HILL.

By special order of the Governor the General Assembly of Connecticut met April 26th. That body voted to organize one-fourth part of the militia of the colony into six regiments for its special defense and safety. As reconstructed the Ashford company, consisting of 100* men, recruited in a town of 2,228 white inhabitants, formed a part of regiment No. 3, Israel Putnam, Colonel. On reaching the field it was stationed at Cambridge, near the headquarters of Gen'l Ward.

---

*Captain, Thomas Knowlton; Lieutenants, John Keyes, Daniel Allen ; Ensign, Squire Hill ; Sergeants, Daniel Eldridge, Obadiah Parry ; Timothy Dimmick, Amos Woodward, and Joseph Snow ; Corporals, David Allen, Daniel Squire, Christopher Bowen, Jedediah Ammidown ; Clerk, Samuel Moseley ; Drummer, Nathaniel Hayward ; Fifer, Benjamin Russell ; Privates, Philip Abbot, Jonathan Avery, William Allen, George Anderson, Stephen Anderson, Thomas Anderson, Isaac Abbe, Amos Bugbee, Joseph Barney, Thomas Bragg (Thomas Bragg taken from a separate roll), Abiel Bugbee, John Broughton, Asaph Burley, Jacob Burley, Thaddeus Brown, Jonathan Badger, Daniel Bosworth, Jonathan Bowen, Joseph Bowen, Lemuel Bowles, Jonathan Chaffee, Jeremiah Connel, Jonathan Crane, Christopher Chapman, Thomas Chapman, William Curtis, William Cheney, Benjamin Dimmick, Thomas Davidson, Asa Davidson, Isaac Dimmick, Amos Dowset, Jonathan Dowset, Timothy Eastman, Josiah Eaton, Daniel Fitts, Stephen Foster, James Grant, Hamilton Grant, Samuel Hale, Caleb Hendee, Benjamin Henfield, Jonathan Holmes, Silas Holt, Josiah Holt, Robert Hale, Charles Kimball, Stephen Knowlton, Zachariah Keyes, Edward Keyes, Fred Knowlton, Asahel Lyon, Amariah Lyon, Jonathan Laflin, Abraham Laflin, Alexander McNall, William Moore, Adin Marcy, Daniel Owen, Jonathan Potter, Robert Patterson, Benjamin Pitts, Zera Preston, Benjamin Russ, Reuben Simmons, James Shepherd, Daniel Smith, Richard Smith, Stephen Scarbrough, Thomas Southworth, Salvanus Snow, Abijah Smith, Josiah Smith, Ebenezer Wales, William Waters, William Watkins, Aaron Wales, Nathaniel Ward, Nathaniel Watkins, Samuel Walker, Eleazer Wales, James Walker, Daniel Ward, Jonathan Woodward, William Williams.

The troops soon wearied of inaction. As weeks wore away with no battle, or skirmish, or achievement of any kind to break the monotony, our people wondered why the gallant generals and colonels, whom they had sent to war amid flaming enthusiasm, should so delay about driving the redcoats into the sea. Though the army was still undisciplined and scantily supplied with munitions, something must be done to quiet the restlessness in camp and at home. Eighty-six years later similar impatience voiced in the cry, "On to Richmond," forced Gen'l Scott to throw his raw levies against the batteries at Bull Run.

If not the originator, Putnam was a strenuous advocate, of the plan of fortifying a position on the peninsula of Charlestown. At the private quarters of Knowlton he unfolded in detail his reasons for the step. But his trusted captain took a different view, arguing that under cover of floating batteries the enemy could land troops at the neck, thus cutting off the garrison from reinforcements and supplies, that the approaches and flanks could be enfiladed from the shipping, and that if successful in throwing up intrenchments the Americans had neither cannon nor ammunition for inflicting any serious injury upon the British. He further contended that by judicious disposal of the land and naval forces at his command Gen'l Gage without bloodshed could speedily starve the expedition into surrender. The sentinel at the door, Edward Keyes, a lad of seventeen, overheard and in after years often repeated the conversation.

A conviction that active measures alone could hush the popular clamor led the Committee of Safety to approve the scheme. If the counselors of boldness counted upon the rashness of the enemy as a factor in the problem, their prescience was justified by results.

PART TAKEN BY THE CONNECTICUT TROOPS.

Two hundred* Connecticut troops selected from six companies and commanded by Knowlton marched with Col. Prescott on the night of June 16th over Bunker's Hill to Breed's Hill, an elevation nearer to the city but not so high. Almost directly east was Moulton's Point, the end of the peninsula. On the south lay the village of Charlestown, resting on the river Charles. On the north at the distance of four hundred yards flowed the Mystic. By daybreak a redoubt about eight rods square had been partially

---

*The detachment was composed of one hundred and twenty men, drafted from the first, second, fourth, and fifth companies of Putnam's regiment; two officers and thirty privates from the company of Capt. Chester; and sixteen men from that of Solomon Willes, both of the Second or Spencer's regiment. Others went with them as volunteers. The number "200" must be treated merely as an estimate.

The orderly book of Capt. Willes, now in possession of Mr. Charles J. Hoadly, under date of June 16th, says:

'Ordered . . . . "that 16 men parade at 6 o'clock P. M., so as to be ready to march from the parade at half past six where they shall be ordered, the men for fatigue to dress as suits their convenience, all others for guard to dress clean and neat with breeches, stockings and shoes, the men to be very punctual at the time for parading."'

The orderly book of Capt. William Coit, published by the Connecticut Historical Society in 1894 makes it clear that his company did not furnish a detail for the night march, as has often been erroneously surmised.

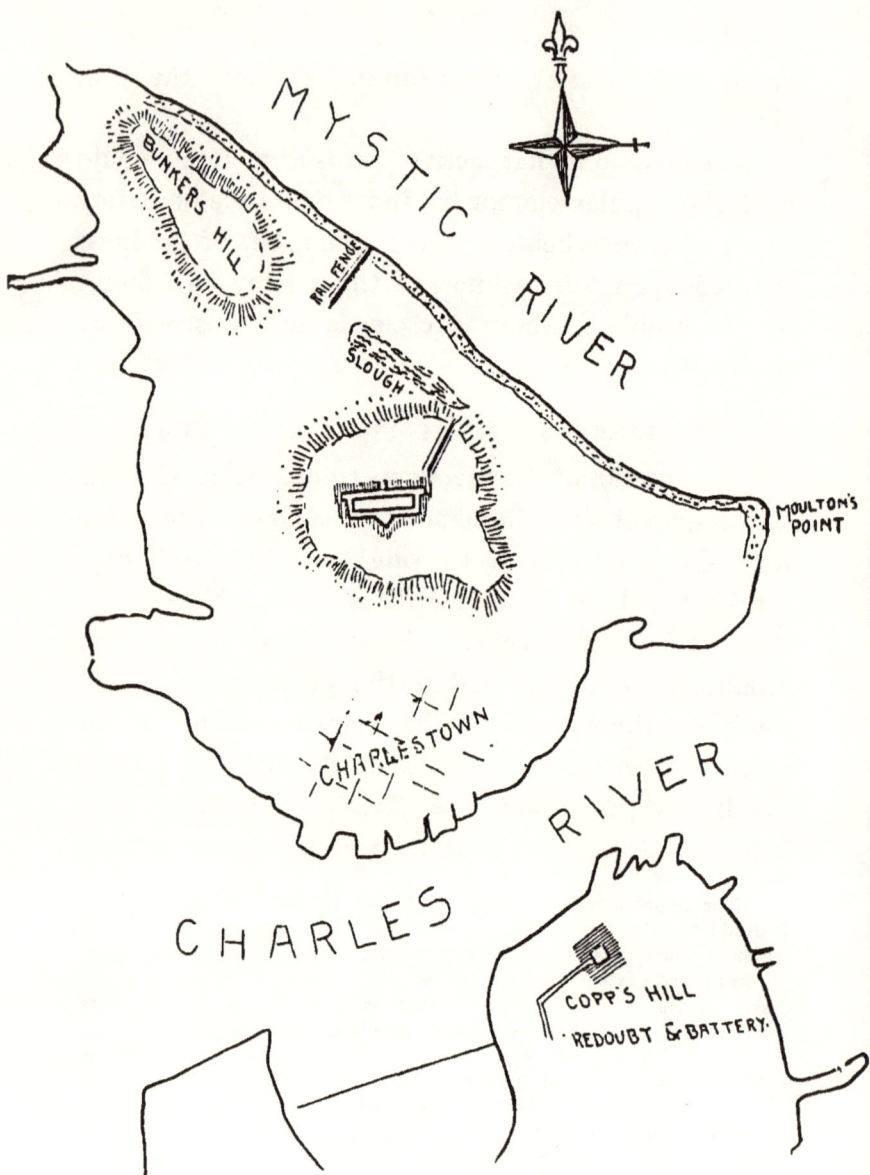

MYSTIC RIVER

BUNKERS HILL

RAIL FENCE

SLOUGH

MOULTON'S POINT

CHARLESTOWN

CHARLES RIVER

COPP'S HILL
REDOUBT & BATTERY

constructed. Then the men-of-war in the harbor
and the battery on Copp's Hill opened upon it. Still
with pick and spade the men toiled on. North of the
redoubt in face of a heavy fire the line was extended
about twenty rods toward a slough at the foot of
the hill.

In the gray of dawn Putnam galloped into
Cambridge to urge upon Gen'l Ward the necessity
of hurrying forward supplies and reinforcements.
Fearing, however, that his own position was to be
attacked, the commander-in-chief was too dazed for
prompt and effective action.

When in the early afternoon the British began to
disembark on the southeastern shore of the peninsula,
Col. Prescott ordered the Connecticut troops in the
redoubt under Knowlton, supported by two field-
pieces, to oppose the landing. The cannon were
nearly useless, as through some blunder the balls
brought to the field did not fit. Had he obeyed the
order a handful of infantry would have marched forth
to sure destruction. At this juncture Knowlton in-
ferred from the movements of Gen'l Howe that it
was his purpose, by advancing along the borders of
the Mystic, to gain the rear of the redoubt and cut
off the retreat of the garrison. Seeing intuitively
the danger and the remedy, he hurried to the critical
point and brought confusion to the plan. Dropping
back about 190 yards to the low ground on the left,
he found a stone fence, surmounted by two rails,
stretching across the fields toward the river. Parallel with this a second rail fence was hastily thrown

up and the interval packed with freshly mown hay. Here the detachment was soon joined by a body of two hundred fresh troops from New Hampshire.

About one o'clock two thousand regulars under Gen'l Howe landed near Moulton's Point, the eastern extremity of the peninsula, where he lost two hours of precious time in waiting for reinforcements. At this juncture the force in the redoubt by details and desertions had been reduced below three hundred. On the plain behind the fence were four hundred more. It looked as if they had been deliberately abandoned. Messenger after messenger sent for food and succor had failed to bring relief. Hungry, thirsty, thirty hours without sleep, worn by severe toil under a hot sun and a still hotter fire of shot and shell, the little band saw the preparations of an army outnumbering them three to one, splendidly equipped, admirably disciplined, hardened by long service and accustomed to victory even when matched against veterans.

During the interval of suspense which followed the landing of the British, a part of Col. Reed's regiment from New Hampshire marched across the neck and took position on the left of Knowlton. Shortly before three o'clock Col. Stark reached the field, when his command filled the gap on the extreme left between Reed and the Mystic. They hastily extended and strengthened the breastwork begun by Knowlton, and threw up a stone wall across the sandy beach from the river bank to the water. Except a few unorganized volunteers who had come to the front from an impulse of personal enthusiasm, these New Hampshire regiments, composed of the best raw material but undisciplined and wretchedly equipped, were the only fresh troops on the field when the action began. The fence line extended about nine hundred feet from the northern slope of Breed's Hill to the Mystic and was defended by about one thousand men. Opposite the north face of the redoubt the hill was skirted by a slough which terminated seventy yards in front of the position held by Knowlton.

While General Pigot with a single column made a demonstration against the redoubt General Howe led two columns along the beach and across the fields that skirted the Mystic with the view of flanking the garrison and cutting off its retreat. He anticipated little resistance from the rustics behind the fence.

Our troops had no powder to spare. Waiting for the approach of the enemy within easy range, and taking deliberate aim, they poured a broad stream of lead into the advancing column. In a few minutes the ground was strewn with the slain, and the broken ranks fell back beyond reach of our guns. A second time they were brought to the charge and a second time were driven back along the whole line from the redoubt to the Mystic. Knowlton, while cheering his men, repeatedly fired his musket till it was knocked into a semicircle by a cannon-ball. He was stunned by the blow and reported killed, but quickly recovered. For a long time the relic was preserved in the family, but like countless other such treasures finally disappeared.

General Clinton, who had thus far watched the engagement from Copp's Hill, saw that from the few ness of its defenders the redoubt, though seemingly the strongest, was in reality the most vulnerable part of the American lines. Crossing the river he held a hurried consultation with General Howe. No record has been preserved of what passed between the two men at that eventful moment. Yet it needs no supernatural gift to divine the essential facts. Around them lay the fragments of a shattered and disheartened army. The day was lost. It might yet be won. Clinton pointed out the way. Hope revived, for does not the courage of the race, on both sides of the Atlantic, rise from direst perils to supremest efforts? General Howe now reversed his plan of battle, making a feint toward the fence to detain its defenders, while an attack from the remnants of his army was concentrated from three sides on the redoubt. One hundred and fifty men, according to the estimate of Colonel Prescott, with little ammunition and fifty bayonets met the onset with unavailing heroism. For a moment before the deadly aim of our marksmen the regulars wavered, and then, as the firing died away from lack of powder, rushed forward with fixed bayonets. Prescott ordered a retreat, his men defending themselves with stones and clubbed muskets as they withdrew.

The abandonment of the fort at once rendered untenable the position behind the fence. The gill of powder and fifteen bullets doled out to each member of Stark's regiment that morning 'at Medford, were expended. Few had a single charge left. Knowlton's command took to the field forty-eight rounds of ammunition, a part of the home outfit, and were still well supplied. The Connecticut companies of Captains Chester, Coit, and Clark, passing several regiments on the road, came upon the field a few minutes before the break, and took position behind the fence.

The retreat was not a rout. The Connecticut troops, now increased to four hundred, were well disciplined, well drilled, and relatively well equipped. As a consequence they could be held in order in the presence of disaster. They now formed the rear guard of the Americans, and by a renewal of musketry firing checked the advance of the enemy. To this fact at least a dozen members of the Ashford company who were living as late as 1830, uniformly bore witness. From its detail of thirty, William Cheney, Asahel Lyon, and Benjamin Russ were killed. Another member, Robert Hale, slipping from the ranks in the final whirl, discharged with terrible effect into the crowd of pursuers a cannon loaded with all sorts of missiles, and escaped unharmed.

The British lost in killed and wounded 1,054; the Americans 449. With timely reinforcements a rash venture might have ended in a signal victory.

In this incomplete account of the battle we have aimed simply to record the deeds of Knowlton and his command. They labored on the redoubt till the walls were finished. After midday they extemporized the breastwork of rails and hay which was extended later to the Mystic by the troops from New Hampshire.

In the plan of General Howe this was the main point of attack, and against repeated assaults by the flower of the English army, the position was held immovably till made untenable by the withdrawal of Prescott. With ammunition still unexpended they covered the retreat, suffering at this time the chief casualties of the day.

The battle was remarkable for the utter disregard by both sides of plain dictates of prudence, for the obstinate valor of the combatants, and for its moral effect at home and abroad. Till then, with here and there an exception, aggrieved Americans hoped that in some way the colonies would so adjust their differences with the crown as to remain integral parts of the British empire. Independence, before the dream of a few, now became the resolve of ever growing numbers till proclaimed with practical unanimity in the immortal declaration of July 4th, 1776.

In recognition of his services, an admirer in Boston gave Captain Knowlton a gold-laced hat, a gorget,* and a sash.

As the season advanced, Knowlton's company, now brought to a high standard of military discipline, served by common consent as a sort of body guard to Washington, "with whom he was an especial favorite."

---

* The gorget, handsomely engraved, now belongs to a descendant, George T. Chaffee of Rutland, Vt. The sash is still in existence, but has passed out of the family.

NIGHT MARCH TO CHARLESTOWN.

Early in January a deserter reported that several English officers were quartered in Charlestown, in houses that had escaped the fire of June 17th. Knowlton was ordered to capture them and destroy the buildings. Having previously reconnoitered the ground, on the evening of January 8th he led two hundred men across the old mill dam from the peninsula to the main — the only way of ingress or egress, as the neck was strongly garrisoned. Arriving at the guardhouse, he struck down the sentinel before he could sound an alarm. Its occupants were captured. A plan had been arranged to fire the most distant buildings first — a plan reversed in execution through the excitement of some of the party. As the flames shot upward, cannon began to blaze from the British fort on Bunker Hill. With five prisoners our column retraced its steps across the dam, without injury to a man, and without discharging a gun.

The adventure had a comic side. At the theatre in the city a play called the "Blockade of Boston" was entertaining a crowded audience. As the character burlesquing Washington strutted across the stage, attended by a ragged orderly, a real sergeant interrupted the fun with the shout, "The Yankees are attacking Bunker Hill!" This was thought to be a part of the play till General Howe gave the order, "Officers, to your alarm posts!" The show closed abruptly in wild confusion.

Early in 1776 the 20th regiment of the line was organized and recruited largely from the old Connecticut 3d. Benedict Arnold, then absent on the expedition against Quebec, was appointed colonel, but never served. January 1, 1776, John Durkee was appointed lieutenant-colonel, and Thomas Knowlton major. An order from the commander-in-chief, dated Cambridge, February 28, 1776, and directed to James Warren, Esq., Paymaster-General of the Army of the United Colonies, runs thus: . . . . "pay Major Thomas Knowlton Five Hundred dollars equal to one hundred and fifty pounds lawful money, for the purpose of purchasing arms for the use of the 20th regiment of foot under his command in the service of the United Colonies and this shall be your sufficient warrant." Knowlton was then in actual command of the regiment. His book of accounts shows that he also acted as paymaster.

CAMPAIGN AROUND NEW YORK.

Howe evacuated Boston March 17, 1776. Soon after the Connecticut troops started for New York. On the way Knowlton saw his home, his wife, and young children for the last time.

Washington directed the continental forces to rendezvous around New York city, rightly surmising that this would be the next point of attack. June 25th Howe arrived off Sandy Hook. His effective force was soon swollen by reinforcements to 24,000 men, supported by a powerful fleet.

In July one Ephraim Anderson obtained the sanction of Congress to a scheme of his contrivance for the destruction by fire ships of the British fleet

moored under Staten Island. Simultaneously the
camp on the island was to be attacked by detachments
under Mercer and Knowlton. The ideas of Anderson
did not materialize in season to be tested. However,
Knowlton, then stationed at Bergen, and Mercer twice
attempted to surprise the enemy at night. Once they
were prevented by a storm, and once by lack of boats.

August 12, 1776, Knowlton was appointed lieutenant-colonel of the 20th regiment. Just ten days later
the British landed on Long Island. On the 26th, with
one hundred picked men from his own regiment, he
crossed over from Bergen, and was sent forward the
same night to the outposts at Flatbush. General
Washington's force in and around the defenses of
Brooklyn numbered about seven thousand, and General
Howe's twenty-one thousand. By a circuitous night
march, strong flanking columns of the enemy, passing
through the remote and unguarded pass at Jamaica,
gained on the morning of the 27th the flank and rear
of our forces stationed at the lower passes. While the
move was nearing completion our lines were occupied
by an attack in front, designed to be sufficiently serious to prevent retreat. Knowlton was sent to rein-
force Lord Sterling on the extreme right. Suddenly
the firing in that direction ceased. Rightly inferring
that Sterling had surrendered, he at once ordered a
retreat, and thus saved his command. Our army was
surprised, beaten, and driven behind the defenses of
Brooklyn. In killed and wounded the opposing forces
suffered about equally, but the Americans lost heavily
in prisoners.

On the night of the 29th, with masterly prevision and skill, Washington withdrew his entire army from Long Island.

KNOWLTON'S RANGERS.

A few days later was completed the organization of a corps known as the Connecticut, or "Knowlton's Rangers." It was made up of volunteers from five Connecticut, one Rhode Island, and two Massachusetts regiments. The scheme probably originated with General Washington, as the command took orders directly from him, and was closely attached to his person. It was known in advance that the corps was intended for both dangerous and delicate work, and hence it attracted only resolute and adventurous spirits. Among the captains were Stephen Brown * of Woodstock, brave, generous, and loving; Thomas Grosvenor of Pomfret, who fought with Knowlton behind the rail fence at Bunker Hill; and Nathan Hale of Coventry, whose name, for Americans at least, will shine high up and forever on the roll of martyrs.

NATHAN HALE.

After the withdrawal from Brooklyn the commander-in-chief desired information that could be gained only within the lines of the enemy. The selection of a suitable agent was entrusted to Colonel Knowlton. No ordinary soldier would answer. Men of culture, on the other hand, recoil from the work of a spy. Hence, when Knowlton presented the case to

* Stephen Brown, born May 10, 1749, son of Stephen Brown, Senior, and of Mary (Lyon) Brown of Ashford, was probably the Captain Brown of the Rangers.

the chiefs of his more than Spartan band, it is not strange that silence was at first broken only by fresh entreaties from his own lips. At length Hale volunteered, reluctantly, sadly, in the spirit of self-abnegation that now and then through the crust of hard environment reveals the divinity in man and exalts him to the skies. Through all time our youth will be lifted to higher aims by the story of the martyr who, amid frowns and jeers, with a rope around his neck, met death regretting that he had but one life to give for his country.

BRITISH OCCUPY NEW YORK CITY.

With overwhelming resources Sir William Howe now laid plans with impressive deliberations to throttle the nascent republic.

Sunday, September 15th, under a heavy cannonade from five men-of-war, the enemy landed above New York city on East River, near Kip's Bay, our militia abandoning their works in a panic. After the terrible punishment inflicted upon him by our left at Bunker Hill, Howe became notably dilatory in following up success. On more than one occasion the habit saved the American cause from disasters which seemed inevitable. When he and his officers reached the mansion of Robert Murray on the hill which bears the family name, Mrs. Murray invited the party to lunch, and, while they were merrily feasting, General Putnam, with 3,500 men, escaped from the net about to close around them, and, hurrying northward along the Bloomingdale road, within a mile of the gay company, effected a junction with the main body at Harlem Heights.

As darkness closed the operations of the day the British lines extended from Horen's Hook, opposite Hell Gate, across the peninsula two miles to the North River, with both flanks protected by men-of-war. Troops had moved over from Long Island in such numbers that the encampment covered the space between the fourth and eighth mile stones, with the advance near McGowan's Pass on the line of 109th street. A mile and a half northward, around the Point of Rocks at 127th Street, was the advance post of the Americans. Between lay Harlem Plains, skirted by wooded hills. A cold pelting rain beat upon our unsheltered men, and added physical discomfort to mental gloom.

BATTLE OF HARLEM HEIGHTS — DEATH OF KNOWLTON.

Before daybreak the next morning, under orders from Washington, Knowlton with the Rangers set out to learn the position of the British advance. Proceeding cautiously through the woods on Bloomingdale Heights, he halted near the southern end of the ridge and sent forward two men to reconnoiter, with explicit instructions to avoid attracting attention. The scouts discovered a body of the enemy, also early in motion, and, yielding to a mad impulse, discharged their muskets and ran back, chased by a large force. A hot fight followed, the Rangers retreating in an orderly manner to the protection of our advance posts, where a stand was made. While the movement was in progress, Adjutant-General Joseph Reed, who had been sent by Washington to obtain information, joined a party of the Rangers, and, encouraged by their gallant behavior under the fire of an enemy outnumbering them three to one, started for headquarters to ask for reinforcements. On the way he met Washington riding to the front. Almost at the same moment the British light infantry came in sight, and sounded their bugles as if to celebrate the close of a fox chase. Our officers felt that the insult was too deadly to be borne.

With the view of cutting off the pursuing party estimated at three hundred, Washington ordered Knowlton and his Rangers, supported by three companies from Virginia under Major Leitch, to gain their rear, while, to hold their attention, a feigned attack was made in front. Familiar with the ground, Knowlton led his force through the woods on the western slope of the Bloomingdale Ridge. The Virginians took another route under the guidance of General Reed.

At ten o'clock the demonstration in front was made with more than the intended vigor. The enemy fell back 800 feet, and rallied behind a fence, whence they were speedily driven out of the plain up the hillside. By the rapidity of the pursuit the plans of the commander-in-chief were deranged, for the force under Knowlton debouched on the flank instead of the rear of the British. Our column began the attack with the utmost intrepidity. Both sides were reinforced and both fought obstinately till the enemy were driven

back to the vicinity of their own lines. Deeming it
imprudent to venture further, Washington ordered
the recall to be sounded, and the men obeyed, though
reluctantly, for the delight of chasing the redcoats be-
wildered them by its novelty.

The American loss was 17 killed and 53 wounded;
the British 70 killed and 210 wounded. The victory,
the first to break a series of continuous disasters, and
the first of the war won in the open field, largely restored the waning confidence of our troops, but by
the death of Knowlton robbed the country of one of
her most promising soldiers. About noon, while lead-
ing a charge, he was shot through the body. He was
placed tenderly on the horse of General Reed, and
borne from the field, but expired in an hour. His son
Frederick was fighting in the ranks, but reached the
side of his father in time to receive his parting words.

In the general orders of September 17th Washington says: "The gallant and brave Colonel Knowlton,
who was an honor to any country, having fallen yes-
terday, while gallantly fighting," etc. In a letter to
General Schuyler, dated September 20th, he says of
the action: "Our loss, except in that of Colonel
Knowlton, a most valuable and gallant officer, is in-
considerable." In similar strain he speaks of him in
his report to the president of Congress.

Writing to his wife September 17th, General Reed,
after describing the heroic conduct of the troops and
the effect of the action in restoring their spirits and
confidence, adds, but "our greatest loss was a brave
officer from Connecticut, whose name and spirit ought

to be immortalized, one Colonel Knowlton. I assisted him off, and when gasping in the agonies of death all his inquiry was if we had drove the enemy."

Captain Stephen Brown of the Rangers, next in rank to Knowlton, and his immediate successor in command, wrote: "My poor colonel, in the second attack, was shot just by my side. The ball entered the small of his back. I took hold of him, asked him if he was badly wounded. He told me he was, but, says he, 'I do not value my life if we do but get the day.' I then ordered two men to carry him off. He desired me by all means to keep up this flank. He seemed as unconcerned and calm as though nothing had happened to him." *

ESTIMATE OF ASSOCIATES.

John Trumbull, the historical painter, served as aid-de-camp to Washington during the early part of the siege of Boston, and later as brigade major at Roxbury. After the evacuation he went with the army to New York. He showed his estimate of

* After the death of Knowlton the question of continuing the separate organization of the Rangers was seriously discussed. Colonel Robert Magaw of Pennsylvania, then in command at Fort Washington, upon the withdrawal of the main army, urged that they be assigned to him, as they were his chief dependence for the security of his outposts. At the surrender of the fort, November 16, 1776, they were captured with the rest of the garrison. Many of these brave men underwent dreadful sufferings, and several perished in British prison ships.

Captain Stephen Brown escaped by rejoining his regiment (the 20th Continental) a few days after the death of his beloved commander. He was killed by a cannon ball in the defense of Fort Mifflin in 1777. Thomas Grosvenor served during most of the war, and retired with the rank of colonel. He graduated at Yale College in 1765, and studied law. He was elected seven times to the lower and nine times to the upper house of the General Assembly of Connecticut. He was made chief judge of the Windham County Court in 1806. He died in 1825.

Knowlton by giving him a central place in his famous painting, " The Battle of Bunker Hill," * where the figures are so grouped as to present portraits of most of the prominent actors.

When the news reached Ashford, the whole town, it is said, was in tears, so beloved was this generous man, and such lofty hopes had been reared upon his genius for arms.

I have a number of manuscript letters written in 1841-2 by Charles Coffin, who, in 1835, issued a pamphlet of thirty-six pages on the battle of Breed's Hill, and who had diligently sought from survivors information regarding its incidents and actors. Among the officers quoted respecting the character and abilities of Colonel Knowlton are General Henry Dearborn, afterwards Secretary of War, Aaron Burr, and Captain Trafton, a companion on the night march across the dam to Charlestown. These and others speak of Knowlton in the highest terms, both as a soldier and a man. Several pronounced him the most promising officer of his grade in the service. Colonel Burr, who was brought into close relations with him during the summer of 1776, conceived an ardent admiration for his military talents, and toward the close of his brilliant but perverse and darkened life loved to recur to this intimacy of youth. To him Knowlton was a hero capable of forming and executing great designs. He said it was impossible to promote such a man too rapidly, adding that, " if he had had the whole control at the battle of Bunker Hill the result would probably have been more fortunate."

---

* The painting which furnished the model for Mr. Woods, the sculptor, belongs to the Wadsworth Atheneum of Hartford.

The remark is quoted merely to show the depth of impression made by the genius of Knowlton upon a keen and critical mind, that based its conclusions not on the opinions of others but on personal knowledge of the man.

Colonel Knowlton was buried with military honors west of Ninth Avenue, near 143d Street. Over his grave throb the pulses of a rich and mighty city, but till November, 1893, not even a tablet marked the resting place or recalled the services of a hero, who answered to the first cry of a country yet unborn, and who thenceforth in crises of supreme peril was ever found where courage and capacity were most needed.

Washington, in a companionship of nearly fifteen months, had learned to rely with equal confidence upon his judgment in council and his valor on the battlefield. He now sent home Frederick, the eldest son, a boy under sixteen, to care for the widow and seven younger children.

In the cemetery at Warrenville, town of Ashford, a rude cenotaph bears these words: "This monument is erected in memory of Colonel Thomas Knowlton and his wife. That brave colonel, in defense of his country, fell in battle September 16, 1776, at Harlem Heights, Island of New York, age 36 years. Mrs. Anna, the amiable consort of Colonel Knowlton, died May 22, 1808, age 64, and is buried beneath this monument."

Four or five miles from this spot, eighty-five years after the fall of Knowlton, to a grave bedewed by the tears of the nation, were borne to burial under the sorrowing eyes of a great multitude gathered from near and far, amid the wail of dirges and the roar of artillery and the pomp of trailing banners, the remains of his grand-nephew, General Nathaniel Lyon. When the uncle, from whose example the boy drew the inspiration of patriotism and the ambition for a military career, passed away, amid disaster and gloom, his comrades had no time to spare for impressive ceremonies. These rites the fourth generation now performs. Through this statue the state proclaims that the heroism of her sons shall ever be held in grateful remembrance; that in the sweep of time the dearest rewards are held for noble deeds.

THE SCULPTOR AND HIS WORK

[Charles Noël Flagg in Hartford Courant]

IT is an exceedingly difficult matter to write a sketch of Enoch S. Woods, because he has that natural reticence which usually accompanies extreme modesty, and seldom speaks of himself. The story of his life is simply that of a mechanic's struggle to better his condition by the self-development of an inborn artistic genius, and the consequently inevitable battles with discouragement and poverty. In one of those rare moments when he speaks of himself he says: "The changes in my life during the past fifteen years have been so great that it seems like a dream. At times the fight has been so hard that I admit that I have sat low in discouragement. Again, a strong resolve and belief in myself has held me to my task ; but even now I am all uncertain as to whether my life has been worth living or not."

Mr. Woods was born at Lorneville, a small and at that time newly-settled town on the coast of Nova Scotia. His father, an Englishman, and his mother, a Nova Scotian, were pioneers in this new country, and having a large family of children were obliged to struggle through all the chapters of the book of honorable necessity. His mother was a woman of deep feeling and impressionable character and his father was skillful in mechanical construction, being able to build a house or make the family shoes. Thus Mr. Woods inherited those wholesome attributes so important to a sculptor, appreciation of beauty and the mechanical skill necessary to execution. From early childhood he was ever making boats and mills and little images in clay which he dug from a neighboring stream. It is needless to say, perhaps, that these occupations were looked upon with disfavor by his father, who, like the father of many another artist, considered artistic ambition a presage of an inclination toward a mild form of sin.

In 1868, being then twenty years of age. Mr. Woods came to the United States, with no definite idea as to his future, except that he must work for a living. He was ambitious, but so timidly reserved that he did not dare attempt to cope with any difficulties except those to be met in an humble occupation. The predominant idea in his mind was work, and so long as it was honest he was always ready. It is not necessary to say just what he did at first, but a narrow escape from accidental death made him change his occupation and become a mason. In this trade he soon became so proficient that he was given employment in the ornamental parts of important buildings. In 1872 he concluded to settle in Hartford. About this time he excited the admiration of his fellow workmen by his ability as an amateur wood-carver. In his few leisure moments he worked in a small room which he had hired for the purpose, and occasionally sold some original designs which he cast in plaster. In 1877 he finally gave up the trade of mason and turned his attention to sculpture. His equipment was very limited, for he had never had the slightest chance to study in any art school or with any sculptor. As a workman going to and from his daily labor he had often carried one of the various bones of the human figure in his pocket, studying it when he had a chance, and in this way he acquired that knowledge of anatomy which was to serve him so well in after life. Occasional trips to New York and Boston enabled him to see works of art, and looking at these from his own standpoint, unprejudiced by the dogmas of any school, he was able to pick out, and profit by the successes and failures of others. Fond of reading, he helped himself greatly by those books which his good taste led him to read. Books on art he never read, as he soon found that they were of no use except from a literary and historical point of view ; but by general and well-chosen reading he improved his capability to see.

To make the statue of Colonel Knowlton was the first order of any importance that Mr. Woods ever received. With the awful warning presented by several regiments of soldier monuments with which the country is encumbered, the commission having the matter in charge was somewhat reluctant in engaging a sculptor. Mr. Woods submitted several studies which did not quite meet with approval, but he convinced the members of the commission that he was greatly in earnest and also that he had a fund of ability which promised success. No statue was ever more conscientiously constructed than the Knowlton. After modeling it all in clay, which was no light matter, the figure measuring eight feet and one inch, he became dissatisfied with his work, destroyed it and began anew. The second time he vastly improved the movement, and built the figure muscle by muscle until it stood the well-drawn, completed statue that it is to-day. I am not going to criticise this work or make any great claims for it. If any think too highly or too poorly of it, time will regulate their opinion, for I am sure that this statue will permanently stand in the position which has been chosen for it by the commission, because it is worthy of the place. How many statues are there in the country of which this much can be justly said?

A few years ago, when the statue of Israel Putnam, which stands in Bushnell Park, was unveiled, a workman, dinner pail in hand, stopped and eagerly watched, forgetting his work in his anxiety to profit by the lesson which that statue might have for him, and as he walked on he dreamed dreams of other statues, in the making of which he hoped some day to have a hand. This same workman, a little later, was employed on the brick work at the southeast corner of the State Capitol, and laid the interior angle and halfway across over the eastern entrance from the top of the columns to the top of the wall. On the 13th of this month the statue of Colonel Knowlton will be formally presented to the State of Connecticut and will stand within fifty feet of where the mason worked at the interior angle. He will be present at the unveiling and will probably hear himself called a great sculptor and will receive many of the compliments incident to such occasions, but I don't think that he will over-estimate them. He has built a good, honest statue to a Revolutionary hero, and at the same time a statue to his own industry and perseverance. That he will in time build greater statues I ·am sure, for the habit of industry is strong in him. I am also sure that in years to come the citizens of Connecticut, when looking at this statue, will often give with pride the story of the workman and his dinner pail in telling that of the sculptor, Enoch S. Woods.

CHARLES NOËL FLAGG.

New York, November 3, 1895.

MEETING OF THE KNOWLTON FAMILY

A FTER the ceremonies of unveiling, members of the Knowlton family allied by blood or marriage met in the Hall of Representatives. Colonel Julius W. Knowlton of Bridgeport called the assembly to order. Dr. Thomas Knowlton Marcy of Windsor was appointed chairman, and William Herrick Griffith of Albany, N. Y., secretary. It was voted to form a permanent association, with annual reunions. Descendants of the three brothers, John, William, and Thomas, who came to America about 1640, are eligible. The following officers were elected: Hon. Marcus P. Knowlton of Springfield, Mass., President; Thomas K. Marcy, Vice-President; and William H. Griffith, Secretary and Treasurer. Rev. Charles H. W. Stocking, D.D., of East Orange, N. J., who reported that he had already collected a large amount of valuable material, was appointed genealogist and historian. Membership was made conditional upon the payment of a yearly assessment, which is to be used for the present in paying expenses incurred in collecting matter for the family history. A vote of thanks was passed to P. H. Woodward for his efforts in securing the statue and in preparing the history of Colonel Thomas Knowlton. June 17, 1896, anniversary of the battle of Bunker Hill, was fixed as the date of the first in the series of reunions. The selection of a place was left to the executive officers.

PATERNAL LINEAGE OF COL. THOMAS KNOWLTON.

The following genealogy of Col. Thomas Knowlton to the seventh generation, inclusive, was prepared by Doctor Ashbel Woodward, and first published in 1861. A few changes have been made in the order of the children of William⁵ to conform more closely to the order of birth.

Were you to make inquiries among the people of New England generally concerning their ancestry, in nine cases out of ten they would tell you that they were descended from one of three brothers who came over from Old England about the year 16—; and in nine cases out of ten they would be wrong. But it so happens in the Knowlton family that three brothers did actually come to New England and settle in Ipswich; John,¹ William,¹ and Deacon Thomas¹; for both John¹ and Thomas¹ call William¹ their brother; evidence of the most satisfactory character.

The second brother, William¹ Knowlton, was a bricklayer. He married Elizabeth ———. He died in 1654 or 5. The inventory of his estate taken July 17, 1655, was £37 2s. 1d. His debts were £27 14s. 1d. We have his descendants for several generations, but it is not our present purpose to include his branch of the family in this brief sketch.

The third brother, Deacon Thomas¹ Knowlton, was born in 1622. He married, first, Susanna ———. His second wife was Mary Kimball, to whom he was married May 17, 1682. It does not appear that he had children.

On the 19th of Nov., 1678, Deacon Thomas thus writes : "I gave a coat to brother William, and his two boys I keept to scool from the age of 5 to 8 years, and a girl from the age of one & a half years till she was married." He died April 3, 1692, aged 70 years.

(1) John,¹ though the last to be noticed, was the eldest of the three brothers. He took the freeman's oath in 1641, was in Ipswich in 1641, perhaps earlier. He made his will Nov. 29, 1653. He married Margery ———. and had John, Abraham, and Elizabeth.

(2) John,² married Sarah ———. He took the freeman's oath in 1680, and died Oct. 8, 1684. His children were —

(3)   I. WILLIAM,³ b. ———. Lived in Wenham, and had wife Lydia.

(4)   II. JOSEPH,³ b. 1651 ; m. Aug. 14, 1677, Mary Wilson.

(5)   III. SAMUEL,³ b. ———; m. April, 1669, Mary Wilt or Witt.

(6)   IV. NATHANIEL,³ Dea., b. June 29, 1658. He m. May 8, 1682, Deborah Jewett, and d. Sept. 28, 1726; r. Ips-

wich. He was long Town Treasurer, and nine times a representative.

Deacon NATHANIEL.[3] (6) and DEBORAH had —
(7)   I.   NATHANIEL,[4] b. May 3, 1683; m. Feb., 1702-3, Mary Bennett.
(8)   II.   JOHN,[4] b. Dec., 1685.
(9)   III.   JOSEPH,[4] b. April, 168-.
(10)   IV.   ABRAHAM,[4] b. Feb. 27, 1688-9.
(11)   V.   ELIZABETH,[4] b. Sept. 18, 1692.
(12)   VI.   THOMAS,[4] b. Nov. 8, 1702.
(13)   VII.   DAVID,[4] b. May, 1707; m. Feb., 1731-2, Esther Howard. David,[5] son of David,[4] d. Dec. 10, 1732.

NATHANIEL[4] (7) and MARY had —
(14)   I.   MARY,[5] b. June 3, 1704.
(15)   II.   WILLIAM,[5] b. Feb. 8, 1705-6; m. Martha Pinder of Boxford, to whom he was published Feb. 13, 1728. He removed to Ashford, Conn., about 1748; d. Mar. 13, 1753.
(16)   III.   NATHANIEL,[5] b. June 30, 1708.
(17)   IV.   JEREMIAH,[5] b. July 13, 1712; and d. young.
(18)   V.   2D JEREMIAH,[5] b. Aug. 2, 1713.

WILLIAM[5] (15) and MARTHA had —
(19)   I.   MARY,[6] b. ———; m. Ezekiel Tiffany of Ashford, Mar. 9, 1748-9.
(20)   II.   SARAH,[6] b. ———; m. Joshua Kendall of Ashford.
(21)   III.   WILLIAM,[6] b. Aug. 9, 1733; m. Mehitable Eaton of Ashford; d. Jan. 9, 1784.
(22)   IV.   LUCY,[6] b. ———; and d. young.
(23)   V.   LUCY,[6] baptized Feb. 20, 1736; m. Abijah Brooks of Ashford.
(24)   VI.   **DANIEL,**[6] baptized Dec. 31, 1738; m. 1st, Elizabeth Farnham of Ashford, Nov. 3, 1763; m. 2d, Rebecca Fenton of Willington, April 24, 1788. He served through the French war and that of the Revolution. During the last he was commissioned as Lieut.
(25)   VII.   **THOMAS,**[6] baptized Nov. 30, 1740; m. Anna Keyes of Ashford, April 5, 1759. Col. Thomas Knowlton was slain in battle at Harlem Heights, Sept. 16, 1776. Anna, wife of Col. Knowlton, d. May 22, 1808.
(26)   VIII.   PRISCILLA,[6] b. ———.
(27)   IX.   NATHANIEL,[6] baptized Mar. 9, 1745; d. July 19, 1749.

Lieut. Daniel.[6] (24) and Elizabeth had —

(28)   I.   Daniel,[7] b. Dec. 7, 1765 ; m. Betsey Burchard. Was a private from Sept. 8, 1782, to Sept. 8, 1783. He died Feb., 1834 ; he had 7 children, the fourth of whom, son Phineas, died a soldier in the army.

(29)   II.   Elizabeth,[7] b. March 24, 1768 ; m. Frederick Chaffee of Ashford.

(30)   III.   Nathaniel,[7] b. Dec. 24, 1770 ; m. Sarah Leach, and had children : Farnham, Emily A., Hosea, Myron, William, and Nathaniel.

(31)   IV.   Manassah,[7] twin brother of Nathaniel, b. Dec. 24, 1770 ; m. 1st, Lydia Burton, and had children : Oren, Ephraim, Isaac, Orendia, Almira, Maria, George W., and Parmelia ; m. 2d, Elizabeth Card ; m. 3d, Clarissa Cogswell.

(32)   V.   Ephraim,[7] b. Oct. 3, 1773.

(33)   VI.   Martha,[7] b. Feb. 24, 1777 ; m. Charles Brandon of Ashford.

(34)   VII.   Keziah,[7] b. Feb. 9, 1781 ; m. Jan. 3, 1805, Amasa Lyon, Esq., of Ashford. She had 9 children, of whom the seventh was General Nathaniel Lyon, born July 14, 1818, and was killed at the battle of Wilson's Creek, Aug. 10, 1861. He graduated at West Point in 1841, ranking 11th in a class of 52 at time of graduation, and of over 100 at the time of entry in 1837. Prior to our civil conflict he had served with distinction in the Seminole and Mexican wars.

(35) VIII.   Hannah,[7] b. April 19, 1738 ; m. Daniel Knowlton, Esq., and had sons: Miner, Danford, Edwin, and daughters: Amanda, Miriam, and Elvira. Their eldest son, Miner, graduated with honor at West Point, and subsequently was a professor in that institution. Unfortunately he became an invalid in middle life, and hence was unable to take part in the stirring events that followed. Danford, their second son, was for many years a prosperous importer in New York city.

By wife Rebecca had —

(36)   IX.   Erastus Fenton,[7] b. Jan. 29, 1790; m. Waite Windsor of Gloucester, R. I.

(37)   X.   Marvin,[7] b. Sept. 3, 1794 ; m. Calista Leonard, of Stafford, Conn.

Col. Thomas[6] (25) and Anna had —

(38)   I.   Frederick,[7] b. Dec. 4, 1760; d. Oct. 9, 1841. Was in the Ashford Co. from May 6, 1775, to Dec. 10, 1775. He served in the campaign of 1776, and was with his father in the battle at Harlem Heights.

(39)   II.   Sally,[7] b. Nov. 23, 1763 ; m. Samuel Utley, at Ashford, Conn., Dec. 6, 1781; rd. in Ashford, Conn., Dalton and Chesterfield, Mass.; d. March 6, 1852.

(40)   III.   Thomas,[7] b. July 13, 1765 ; was in the army from Aug. 9, 1782, to Aug. 9, 1783 ; m. Martha Marcy of Willington, Conn., —— 1807 ; rd. in Willington ; d. May 2, 1858.

(41)   IV.   Polly,[7] b. Jan. 11, 1767; m. Stephen Fitts of Ashford, Conn., Jan. 1, 1793; d. Sept. 27, 1845.

(42)   V.   Abigail,[7] b. June 20, 1768; m. Thomas Chaffee of Ashford, Conn., Nov. 21, 1791; rd. in Becket, Mass.; d. Sept. 18, 1843.

(43)   VI.   Sampson,[7] b. Feb. 8, 1770; d. Sept. 10, 1777.

(44)   VII.   Anna,[7] b. June 8, 1771; d. June 4, 1772.

(45)   VIII.   Anna,[7] b. Mar. 19, 1773; m. Dr. John Kittredge, Jan. 1, 1804; d. June 19, 1817; rd. in Ashford.

(46)   IX.   Lucinda,[7] b. Nov. 10, 1776; d. Feb. 16, 1805.

Sally Knowlton[7] (39) and Samuel Utley had —

(47)   I.   Sally,[8] b. July 18, 1782, in Ashford ; d. young.

(48)   II.   Polly,[8] b. Feb. 10, 1784, in Ashford ; m. Gershom House of Chesterfield, 1803 ; d. Sept. 13, 1858.

(49)   III.   Frederick,[8] b. in Dalton (?), April 24, 1787 ; m. Cynthia Ludden, April 25, 1816 ; r. in Chesterfield ; d. in Westfield, Mass., April 5, 1856.

(50)   IV.   William,[8] b. in Dalton (?) ; r. in Chesterfield ; d. in Williamsburg, Mass., Dec. 28, 1871, aged 82 years ; unmarried ; was a soldier in the war of 1812.

(51)   V.   Sally,[8] b. in Dalton (?) ; r. in Chesterfield ; d. July 12, 1846, aged 54 years ; unmarried.

(52)   VI.   James,[8] b. in Dalton (?) ; r. in Chesterfield ; d. Dec. 4, 1817, aged 24 years ; unmarried.

(53)   VII.   Ralph,[8] b. in Dalton (?) ; m. Zeruah Baker ; r. in Chesterfield and Goshen ; d. Nov. 7, 1862, aged 66 yrs., 7 mos., without children.

(54)   VIII.   Samuel,[8] b. in Dalton (?), Feb. 19, 1798 ; m. Mary J. Eastman, April 14, 1834 ; d. Aug. 20, 1883 ; clergyman.

(55)   IX.   Thomas Knowlton,[8] b. in Chesterfield, Mar. , 1804 ; m. Theodocia Knox of Blandford, Mass., Jan. 18, 1834 ; r. in Chesterfield ; d. Nov. 6, 1847.

POLLY UTLEY [5] (48) and GERSHOM HOUSE had (all born in Chesterfield, Mass.) —

(56)   I. ALMIRA,[9] b. Feb. 14, 1804; m. Holly Bryant; r. in Chesterfield; d. June 10, 1889.

(57)   II. JULIA,[9] b. June 15, 1807; m. George D. Taylor; r. Feeding Hills, Mass.; d.

(58)   III. SAMUEL,[9] b. April 8, 1810; m. Clara R. Johnson, June 20, 1838; r. Chesterfield and Haydenville, Mass.

(59)   IV. LUCINDA,[9] b. Nov. 16, 1812; m. Levi Clapp, April 15, 1835; r. Chatham Centre, Ohio.

(60)   V. BENJAMIN,[9] b. April 25, 1815; m. Frances Warner; r. Greenwich, Mass.; d.

(61)   VI. ANNA K.,[9] b. Aug. 14, 1817; m. Lyman Root; r. Westfield, Mass.; d. Nov. 2, 1882.

(62)   VII. JAMES,[9] b. Jan. 11, 1821; m. Harriet Northrop; r. Westfield, Mass.

(63)   VIII. AMELIA,[9] b. April 9, 1823; m. Chas. Cushing, May —, 1850; r. San Francisco, Cal.

(64)   IX. MARIA,[9] b. June 10, 1825; m. George Cook, Dec. 25, 1852; r. Oberlin, Ohio.

(65)   X. MARIETTA,[9] b. Feb. 4, 1828; m. Oliver Edwards, Jr.; r. in Chesterfield; d. Aug. 8, 1864.

FREDERICK UTLEY [5] (49) and CYNTHIA had (all b. in Chesterfield, Mass.) —

(66)   I. SARAH,[9] b. July 17, 1817; m. Enoch A. Root, May 30, 1839; r. in Westfield, Mass.; d. Feb. 3, 1890.

(67)   II. MARY A,[9] b. Aug. 31, 1819; m. Charles J. Leonard, Oct. 26, 1842; r. in Springfield, Mass.

(68)   III. AMELIA,[9] b. Dec. 20, 1821; m. Francis S. Eggleston, May 22, 1845; res. in Westfield, Mass.; d. Aug. 15, 1893.

(69)   IV. JAMES,[9] b. Jan. 26, 1824; d. Sept. 16, 1825.

(70)   V. AMANDA M.,[9] b. Jan. 13, 1828; m. Stephen B. Cook, Nov. 25, 1849; r. in Westfield, Mass.

(71)   VI. ZERUAH,[9] b. Sept. 9, 1833; m. Charles Deuel, Jan. 17, 1854; r. in Amherst, Mass.

SAMUEL UTLEY [5] (54) and MARY J. had —

(72)   I. SARAH LEE,[9] b. at Epping, N. H., Dec. 19, 1835; m. Aug. 10, 1859, Simeon F. Woodin; r. in Springfield, Mass.

(73)   II. JULIA M.,[9] b. at Chesterfield, Mass., Nov. 27, 1837; m. Aug. 10, 1859, William C. Bailey; d. in Washington, D. C., March 21, 1894.

4

(74)　III.　James,[3] b, July 13, 1840, in New Marlborough, Mass.;
　　　　m. Mar. 26, 1861, Martha F. Dunlap ; r in Taunton
　　　　and Newton, Mass.; physician.

(75)　IV.　Mary J.,[9] b. May 27, 1846, in New Marlborough,
　　　　Mass.; m. Oct. 14, 1868, J. Wesley Jones ; r. in
　　　　Chatham, N. Y.

Thomas Knowlton Utley [8] (55) and Theodocia had (all born in
　　　　Chesterfield, Mass.) —

(76)　I.　Elizabeth,[9] b. Mar. 12, 1835 ; m. George Stephenson,
　　　　June 14, 1853 ; r. in Goshen and Northampton, Mass.

(77)　II.　Adelaide,[9] b. Jan. 13, 1838; d. Sept. 6, 1856.

(78)　III.　Mary J.,[9] b. Jan. 4, 1841 ; r. in Conway, Mass.

(79)　IV.　Samuel,[9] b. Sept. 29, 1843 ; m. Julia M. Martin, Dec.
　　　　8, 1875 ; r. in Worcester, Mass.; judge.

(80)　V.　Thomas Knowlton,[9] b. Sept. 20, 1846 ; m. Octavia
　　　　H. Bates, Jan. 1, 1868 ; r. in Chesterfield, Mass.

Thomas Knowlton [7] (40) and Martha had —

(81)　I.　Martha,[8] b. Dec. 14, 1811 ; m. William W. Marcy,
　　　　————, 1832; d. Sept. 8, 1884.

(82)　II.　Thomas M.,[8] b. Sept. 10, 1808; d. July 5, 1811.

Martha Knowlton [8] (81) and William W. Marcy had, born in
　　　　Willington, Conn. —

(83)　I.　Hannah,[9] b. May 3, 1833; m. Darius Starr of Willing-
　　　　ton, May 8, 1858; d. March 24, 1893.

(84)　II.　Thomas Knowlton,[9] b. Jan. 9, 1835 ; m. 1st, Mary G.
　　　　Hatheway of Windsor, Conn., May 17, 1865; m. 2d,
　　　　Ellen M. Hatheway, June 11, 1884.

(85)　III.　Martha K.,[9] b. June 26, 1841; m. Thomas Chaffee of
　　　　Brooklyn, N. Y., Nov. 24, 1870.

(86)　IV.　Lucy E.,[9] b. Nov. 29, 1848 ; m. Sidney W. Crofut of
　　　　Brooklyn, N. Y., June 9, 1870.

(87)　V.　Matthew,[9] b. April — 1855; d. May 3. 1858.

Polly Knowlton [7] (41) and Stephen Fitts had, born in Ashford —

(88)　I.　Christian,[8] b. Aug. 11, 1794; m. William Loomis,
　　　　Sept. 14, 1817; d. March 13, 1879.

(89)　II.　Stephen Jr.,[8] b. Oct. 29, 1798 ; m. Waty Moore, Nov.
　　　　24, 1830; d. Oct. 23, 1875.

(90)　III.　Maria,[8] b. July 18, 1802; m. Selden Moseley, Oct. 11,
　　　　1832 ; d. April 29, 1889.

(91)　IV.　Thomas Knowlton,[8] b. July 11, 1807; d. Feb. 7, 1831,
　　　　unmarried.

CHRISTIAN FITTS⁻ (SS) and WILLIAM LOOMIS had, born in Ashford —
(92)   I.   MARY ANN,⁹ b. Jan. 29, 1820 ; r. in Ashford.
(93)   II. CHESTER,⁹ b. Feb. 8, 1822; d. Oct. 1, 1874.

STEPHEN FITTS, JR.⁻ (89) and WATY had, born in Ashford —
(94)   I.   THOMAS KNOWLTON,⁹ b. Oct. 23, 1831 : r. in Hartford.
(95)   II. JOHN S.,⁹ b. May 12, 1839; m. 1st, Josephine M. Chap-
            man of Ashford, Nov. 25, 1868; m. 2d, Ellen L.
            James of Tolland, Conn., Oct. 3, 1882 ; r. in Ash-
            ford.
(96)   III. GEORGE H.,⁹ b. April 10, 1843.
(97)   IV. MARY C.,⁹ b. Feb. 21, 1845 ; m. Chas. J. Gifford of
            Ashford, Sept. 29, 1868; r. in Willimantic, Conn.

MARIA FITTS⁸ (90) and SELDEN MOSELY had, born in Ashford —
(98)   I.   NATHAN JAMES,⁹ b. Aug. 29, 1833; m. Betsey Ames of
            New London, Conn., Nov. 29, 1858; r. in New Lon-
            don.

ABIGAIL KNOWLTON⁷ (42) and THOMAS CHAFFEE had —
(99)   I.   SAMPSON KNOWLTON,⁸ b. Aug. 4, 1792; d. Feb. 19, 1813.
(100) II. FREDERICK,⁸ b. Nov. 25, 1793; d. Feb. 13, 1816.
(101) III. WOLCOTT,⁸ b. May 3, 1795; m. Abigail Kingsley, Apr.
            22, 1818; d. Nov. 25, 1870.
(102) IV. NEWMAN K.,⁹ b. Dec. 15, 1796 ; m. 1st, Elizabeth
            Phelps, March 15, 1820; m. 2d, Olive Abbott, March
            1, 1837; d. in West Becket, Mass., Dec. 15, 1858.
(103) V.   MINER,⁸ b. Feb. 6, 1799; m. Lucy Frary, June 9, 1825;
            d. Sept. 29, 1880.
(104) VI. ALMA,⁸ b. Feb. 9, 1801; m. Wm. P. Hamblin, Nov. 8,
            1830; d. in Lee, Mass., March 6, 1838.
(105) VII. ANNA H.,⁻ b. Feb. 4, 1803 ; m. Justin M. Ames, Jan.
            20, 1824; d. Aug. 17, 1859.
(106) VIII. THOMAS S.,⁸ b. March 24, 1805; m. 1st, Betsey Shaw,
            Feb. 4, 1829 ; m. 2d, Lucy Culver, Jan. 3, 1832 ; m.
            3d, Catharine L. Blair, Nov. 2, 1843; d. Oct. 7, 1874.
(107) IX. LUCINDA,⁸ b. Jan. 12, 1807 ; m. Kendall Baird of
            Becket, Mass., Oct. 10, 1827; d. April 1, 1863.
(108) X.   PRENTISS,⁸ b. Jan. 1, 1809 ; m. Betsey Cannon, April
            15, 1833; d. April 10, 1892.
(109) XI. ABIGAIL H.,⁸ b. April 12, 1811; m. Wm. Clark, Jan. 8,
            1833; d. ———.
(110) XII. SAMPSON KNOWLTON,⁸ b. July 11, 1814 ; m. Amelia
            Shaylor, Jan. 27, 1839; d. Nov. 19, 1891.

NEWMAN K. CHAFFEE [8] (102) and Elizabeth had —
(111)   I.   EBENEZER,[9] b. Dec. 12, 1820.
(112)   II. FREDERICK,[9] b. March 17, 1823 ; m. Charlotte Thrall,
             Oct. 31, 1850; d. April 21, 1891.
(113)   III. WOLCOTT,[9] b. June 15, 1826; m. Jennette Judd, July
             8, 1849.
(114)   IV. JOSEPH C.[8], b. Aug. 19, 1828; m. Caroline L. Phelps,
             Nov. 30, 1859.
(115)   V.   ELIZABETH ANN,[9] b. Oct. 5, 1831; m. William Alson
             Messenger, Sept. 26, 1852.
By wife OLIVE had —
(116)   VI. LUCRETIA,[9] b. Dec. 12, 1839.

MINER CHAFFEE [8] (103) and LUCY had —
(117)   I.   HENRY,[9] b. April 9, 1826 ; m. Charlotte Carter, June
             24, 1870.
(118)   II. SARAH,[9] Feb. 4, 1829 ; m. Jonathan W. Wheeler, Aug.
             15, 1850.
(119)   III. EMMA,[9] b. Feb. 27, 1833 ; d. June 14, 1892.
(120)   IV. THOMAS,[9] b. Dec. 31, 1838 ; m. Martha Knowlton
             Marcy, Nov. 24, 1870.

ALMA CHAFFEE [8] (104) and WILLIAM P. HAMBLIN had —
(121)   I.   WILLIAM H.,[9] b. Aug. 30, 1831.

ANNA H. CHAFFEE [8] (105) and JUSTIN M. AMES had —
(122)   I.   SAMANTHA M.,[9] b. Dec. 24, 1826 ; m. Joshua Barnard,
             Feb. 1, 1847.
(123)   II. ZERUAH,[9] b. Oct. 6, 1828 ; m. Joseph Osborn, Mar. 4,
             1852.
(124)   III. SAMPSON CHAFFEE,[9] b. July 28, 1830 ; m. Sarah Haw-
             kins, Sept. 12, 1861.
(125)   IV.* GEORGE LUTHER,[9] b. July 16, 1832 ; m. Ellen L.
             Tinker, May 16, 1855.
(126)   V.   LUCY ANN,[9] b. Oct. 6, 1834 ; m. Nelson D. Gibbs, July
             1, 1852.
(127)   VI. LUCINDA,[9] b. Mar. 6, 1837 ; m. Jas. P. Meacham, June
             25, 1862.
(128)   VII. THOMAS MINER,[9] b. July 20, 1839 ; m. 1st, Emily Rose,
             April 18, 1866; m. 2d, Irene Cowen, Mar. 11, 1884 ;
             d. Jan. 13, 1893.
(129)   VIII. WILSON,[9] b. April 16, 1841 ; m. Abigail R. Wilcox,
             April 28, 1867.
(130)   IX. JULIA ELIZA,[9] b. Mar. 24, 1843.
(131)   X.   FRANKLIN,[9] b. July 7, 1845 ; m. Emma Cowen, July
             11, 1876.

THOMAS S. CHAFFEE[8] (106) and CATHARINE L. had —
(132) I. SHERMAN B.,[9] b. Sept. 2, 1844; m. Alice Williams,
Nov. 20, 1882; d. Feb. 29, 1892.
(133) II. THEODORE W.,[9] b. Jan. 23, 1847; m. Harriet P. Stowe,
Aug. 14, 1873.
(134) III. EDWARD C.,[9] b. July 21, 1850; d. Sept. 11, 1852.
(135) IV. FREDERICK KNOWLTON,[9] b. May 9, 1855.

LUCINDA CHAFFEE[8] (107) and KENDALL BAIRD had —
(136) I. ABIGAIL E.,[9] b. ——, 1828; m. H. C. Wilson; d. ——,
1891.
(137) II. PRENTISS C.,[9] b. ——, 1831; d. ——, 1890.
(138) III. ALMA L.,[9] b. ——, 1834; m. Nathaniel Kellogg, ——,
1853.
(139) IV. CATHARINE A.,[9] b. ——, 1838; m. Lloyd Caul, ——,
1867.
(140) V. FREDERICK KNOWLTON,[9] b. ——, 1842; m. 1st. Caroline Clark, ——, 1862; m. 2d, Jeanette Clark, ——,
1868.
(141) VI. GEORGE K,[9] b. ——, 1846; m. F. Isabel Hitchcock,
——, 1869.

PRENTISS CHAFFEE[8] (108) and BETSEY had —
(142) I. GEORGE L.,[9] b. Sept. 30, 1834; m. Constance Hender-
son, May 16, 1865.
(143) II. MARY E.,[9] b. Mar. 16, 1840; m. Joseph Warren, Nov.
29, 1866.

SAMPSON KNOWLTON CHAFFEE[8] (110) and AMELIA had —
(144) I. CHARLES S.,[9] b. Dec. 13, 1837; m. Martha B. George,
May, —, 1861; d. Jan. 16, 1876.

SKETCH OF THE UTLEY ANCESTRY.

By SAMUEL UTLEY of Worcester, Mass.

—

William Hatch, merchant, came from Sandwich, Eng., to Scituate, Mass., March 17, 1634, with wife, 6 children, and 6 servants. He became ruling elder of the church.

Samuel Utley, of Scituate, was made a freeman between 1643–57.

Samuel m. Hannah, dau. of Elder Wm. Hatch, Dec. 6, 1658 ([1])

Lydia, b. Dec. 28, 1659.

His estate settled, June —, 1662.

He probably had son, Samuel, the record of whose birth is lost.

Samuel and Lydia appear in Stonington, Conn., where their mother had relatives.

Lydia m. Geo. Hewitt, June —, 1683.

Numerous entries refer to Samuel, land being set off to him, July 7, 1682.

Samuel m. Sarah Asbee, April 9, 1691.

They had 8 children, the third, James, b. Sept. 24, 1695.

James was deacon and Capt. in Windham ; m. Annah ———, perhaps in Norwich.

They had 9 children b. in Windham, the second, Samuel, b. May 28, 1723.

Samuel m. Hannah Abbott, Aug. —, 1748.

They had 13 children, the sixth, Samuel, b. Feb. 2, 1759 ; d. Aug. 17, 1828.

Samuel m. (39) Sally, dau. of Col. Thomas Knowlton, Dec. 6, 1781.

Samuel Utley was in the 20th Continental Regiment from Conn., was at the sieges of Boston and New York, at Fort Lee and the retreat in N. J., was at the battles of Trenton and Princeton (?), was in the 1st Regiment Conn. Line, July 1, 1780, to Dec. 9, 1780, was, perhaps, in Wolcott's Regiment and Meade's Regiment for short terms under the name of Samuel Sutley.

———

([1]) Many books erroneously give 1648 ; this is from personal examination of the *original* town record.

www.ingramcontent.com/pod-product-compliance
Lightning Source LLC
Chambersburg PA
CBHW031803090426
42739CB00008B/1136